A GIRL IN A CAR WITH A MAN

by Robert Alan Evans

Copyright © 2020 by Robert Alan Evans
All Rights Reserved

A GIRL IN A CAR WITH A MAN is fully protected under the copyright laws of the British Commonwealth, including Canada, the United States of America, and all other countries of the Copyright Union. All rights, including professional and amateur stage productions, recitation, lecturing, public reading, motion picture, radio broadcasting, television and the rights of translation into foreign languages are strictly reserved.

ISBN 978-0-573-13217-9

concordtheatricals.co.uk
concordtheatricals.com

FOR AMATEUR PRODUCTION ENQUIRIES

UNITED KINGDOM AND WORLD
EXCLUDING NORTH AMERICA
licensing@concordtheatricals.co.uk
020-7054-7200

Each title is subject to availability from Concord Theatricals, depending upon country of performance.

CAUTION: Professional and amateur producers are hereby warned that *A GIRL IN A CAR WITH A MAN* is subject to a licensing fee. Publication of this play does not imply availability for performance. Both amateurs and professionals considering a production are strongly advised to apply to the appropriate agent before starting rehearsals, advertising, or booking a theatre. A licensing fee must be paid whether the title is presented for charity or gain and whether or not admission is charged.

This work is published by Samuel French Ltd, an imprint of Concord Theatricals.

The Professional Rights in this play are controlled by Casarotto Ramsay, 7 Savoy Court, The Strand, London WC2R 0EX.

No one shall make any changes in this title for the purpose of production. No part of this book may be reproduced, stored in a retrieval system, or transmitted in any form, by any means, now known or yet to be invented, including mechanical, electronic, photocopying, recording, videotaping, or otherwise, without the prior written permission of the publisher. No one shall upload this title, or part of this title, to any social media websites.

The right of Robert Alan Evans to be identified as author of this work has been asserted in accordance with Section 77 of the Copyright, Designs and Patents Act 1988.

MUSIC USE NOTE

Licensees are solely responsible for obtaining formal written permission from copyright owners to use copyrighted music in the performance of this play and are strongly cautioned to do so. If no such permission is obtained by the licensee, then the licensee must use only original music that the licensee owns and controls. Licensees are solely responsible and liable for all music clearances and shall indemnify the copyright owners of the play(s) and their licensing agent, Concord Theatricals, against any costs, expenses, losses and liabilities arising from the use of music by licensees. Please contact the appropriate music licensing authority in your territory for the rights to any incidental music.

IMPORTANT BILLING AND CREDIT REQUIREMENTS

If you have obtained performance rights to this title, please refer to your licensing agreement for important billing and credit requirements.

USE OF COPYRIGHT MUSIC

A licence issued by Concord Theatricals to perform this play does not include permission to use the incidental music specified in this copy. Where the place of performance is already licensed by the PERFORMING RIGHT SOCIETY (PRS) a return of the music used must be made to them. If the place of performance is not so licensed then application should be made to the PRS, 2 Pancras Square, London, N1C 4AG. A separate and additional licence from PHONOGRAPHIC PERFORMANCE LTD, 1 Upper James Street, London W1F 9DE (www.ppluk.com) is needed whenever commercial recordings are used.

FIRST PERFORMANCE

A Girl In A Car With A Man was first performed at the Royal Court in 2004. The director was Joe Hill Gibbins, with design by Ultz, lighting design by Johanna Towan and Ultz, and sound by Paul Arditti. The cast was as follows:

ALEX	Andrew Scott
STELLA	Claudie Blakley
DAVID	Mark Bonnar
PAULA	Sukie Smith
POLICEMAN	Mark Leadbetter

CHARACTERS

ALEX
STELLA
DAVID
PAULA
POLICEMAN

Darkness.

Over everything, a film plays. It is the grainy footage from a CCTV camera. A girl playing in the street. The low light of an autumn afternoon comes through the trees. A man takes the girl by the hand and leads her to a car. She gets in the passenger seat, the car drives off. The film plays again. Fades.*

Darkness.

We see **STELLA** *driving. The glow of the dashboard on her face. There are rhythms around her body. The beat of the rain on the car. The wash of the windscreen wipers, the clunk of the road beneath.*

ALEX *is lit bright with the neon lights of a tube train.*

PAULA *is lit by a CCTV monitor, her eyes flicker, taking in every detail.*

DAVID *is lit by a single lamp. In front of him are the parts of an old transistor radio.*

The sounds of a radio being tuned in.

RADIO Heavy downpours will continue across the country and well into tonight, floods are predicted across many areas as rainfall levels reach their highest since nineteen seventy-six...

Static.

---

*A licence to produce *A Girl In A Car With A Man* does not include a performance license for any third-party or copyrighted recordings. Licensees should create their own.

RADIO ...Another from the legendary Charlie Parker in tonight's non-stop jazz hour...

Static.

Radio 4 pips.

Static.

*The hot sound of a trumpet squealing.**

Static.

Well, it was only after fifteen years I realised what was going on, where all the light was going, somewhere in the universe there was a stellar explosion and I was feeling it in my dreams, picking up on it...

Static.

The sound of the trumpet again, a long high note. It sounds like the screech of brakes.*

Simultaneously the light flickers out on **ALEX**, *snaps out on* **DAVID** *and* **STELLA**.

---

*A licence to produce *A Girl In A Car With A Man* does not include a performance license for any third-party or copyrighted music. Licensees should create an original composition or use music in the public domain. For further information, please see Music Use Note on page iii.

1.

The rain is washing over fields and over a cottage. Quite ramshackle.

We can hear the rain beating off the tiles on the roof and gushing down drains.

DAVID, *wearing a woollen jumper that is too big for him, is standing in front of* **STELLA**, *whose hair is plastered to her face and to her shoulders. She is deathly pale and shivering.*

DAVID You.

STELLA I...I saw the light here.

I'm sorry.

There's been an accident.

DAVID *is silent.*

On the road.

Can I come in?

DAVID *moves to let her in.*

I was fiddling, trying to get some music.

DAVID *is silent.*

It's raining.

DAVID Yes.

STELLA I hate jazz.

DAVID I didn't realise.

STELLA It was non-stop; the man said it could go on all night.

DAVID It's pouring.

STELLA So I reached out without taking my eyes off...all that rain, I couldn't see.

DAVID I didn't hear it.

STELLA And I must have hit the wrong button because all of a sudden it's twice as loud. There's a button that does that. I don't use it.

DAVID *(to himself)* It's pouring. How could you not notice that?

STELLA A trumpet, screaming, solo, I've never heard anything like it.

DAVID Like what?

STELLA I took my eyes off for a second, just to get rid of it. I mean I wouldn't have minded just switching the whole thing off, I'd reached that point where I wouldn't have minded, but I couldn't see the right button at first... Should've punched it.

DAVID Punched it?

STELLA Should've punched it into the dashboard.

I'm staring right at it and I still couldn't find the button, hadn't done it, but I look up, because you do don't you...after you've looked down a certain time, you get nervous. So I look up and...there's someone in the road.

DAVID What?

STELLA ...

DAVID You hit someone?

STELLA ...I don't know.

2.

ALEX – *a young man, striking-looking, like he'd smile at you in a bar and you wouldn't know if it was good or bad.*

ALEX Rattle. Rattle. Rattle.

My body is against some poor girl whose face is likewise up against the armpit of a businessman.

No doubt he's pressed against fellows and ladies and we're all rattling along together.

Dead.

Comfortable like.

The carriage filled with the stale and tired smell of office workers.

Normal.

Normal Friday.

Except for me.

Except for me feeling a bit...opulent.

One cute boy, medium build.

Hairy.

Notices my stare.

I can't resist.

"I want to fuck you" I mouth at him.

Slow like.

Obvious.

Bad.

Unfortunately a screech in the carriage and the white flash of metal on metal light me up. Far too dramatic.

Me standing staring, mouthing.

Scares him.

See it in his eyes.

Scared.

Should've had him on the floor, his back to the rails, speeding along and looking up at me.

Should've had him. Looking up at me.

The girl I'm resting against twists her neck and stares at me. My half-erection pressing on her back.

Smiles at me.

Sinister.

Something wild in her eyes.

3.

A closed-circuit television control room. It is dimly lit. There are no windows. **PAULA** *comes to the end of a tape she has been watching.* She is obviously tired. Her phone goes. She takes it out, looks at it and then puts it to silent, placing it on the table beside her. She watches it until it stops and the light has gone off.*

---

*A licence to produce *A Girl In A Car With A Man* does not include a performance license for any third-party or copyrighted recordings. Licensees should create their own.

4.

DAVID *and* STELLA, *the living room.* DAVID *is wet.*

DAVID Nothing.

STELLA What?

DAVID There was nothing out there.

STELLA Oh.

You're soaked.

DAVID I know.

STELLA Take those things off, I'll get a towel.

DAVID What about your car?

STELLA What about it?

DAVID You were driving.

STELLA Yes. But you just said there was nothing?

DAVID No.

STELLA Well then.

You'll catch your death. Come on.

DAVID I'm okay.

STELLA No one likes a summer cold, it's inappropriate.

DAVID It's October.

STELLA Don't be clever.

DAVID I thought there'd be something there.

STELLA Like what?

DAVID Skid marks. Tyre tracks. Broken glass.

STELLA But there wasn't?

DAVID No.

STELLA Maybe they were washed away.

DAVID I'll phone the police.

STELLA I've done that. I've phoned them. They said to hold tight, they said they'd come straight out.

...

Only they were quite busy.

DAVID Busy!?

STELLA They said there was flooding. They said people were floating out the windows.

Not literally.

DAVID Someone could be hurt.

STELLA There are sandbags.

DAVID I mean someone could be hurt, out there.

STELLA Right.

DAVID Did you tell them that? Did you tell them about the crash?

STELLA No.

DAVID You were shocked. I'll phone them again.

He picks up the phone.

STELLA Actually...listen...that's what I wanted to say. When you were gone, well, I had some time to think it through...it's a lovely place and I just sat here and I went over it again, you know, sort of replayed it and do you know I don't think I've been telling it quite right.

DAVID What?

STELLA Well, when I thought about it I realised it was just me. On the road. I guess I wasn't looking properly. And all the water coming down the windscreen like that, I made a mistake, it was like a river, easy to slip. So we slipped.

DAVID We?

STELLA Me and the car.

DAVID I couldn't see a car.

STELLA Well, it's dark blue. It's almost black.

DAVID I couldn't see it.

STELLA So you keep saying, and I'm agreeing, I'm not surprised.

DAVID I could've been looking in the wrong place. They could be lying there. I should go again.

STELLA I was daydreaming. I was thinking of things. That's all. And that fucking radio.

When I looked up I thought I saw something that wasn't there. Have you never done that?

DAVID No.

STELLA Well, good for you.

DAVID stares at her.

Look. Calm down. Have a seat.

DAVID Yes.

He stays standing.

I don't know what we're meant to do.

STELLA We wait for the police and then they'll take my details and probably yours and... I don't know, I've never done this before.

DAVID I didn't even know it was raining. I should've known that. I was just fixing the radio and then...when I went out there it's all changed. All gone. I thought, 'Where's it all gone?' Underwater.

STELLA So, what's your name? Just to practice. They'll probably ask you that.

DAVID David.

STELLA Dave? Davie? You like either of those?

DAVID No.

STELLA Single? Married? Divorced?

DAVID I –

STELLA Single.

DAVID Look / are you sure...

STELLA Height...five eleven, medium build, brown eyes, age... late thirties.

DAVID What are you doing?

STELLA Practicing. Description.

DAVID You said you hit someone.

STELLA I didn't.

DAVID You said someone was in the road.

STELLA Did I? Yes. Yes I did say that.

...

...

It was just me. Really. I drift sometimes, you know. And the rain. I mean listen to that. Listen to it.

How could you not notice that?

5.

ALEX Shower, bubbles in my hair, bubbling and rattling off the skin on my back.

Hand leisurely over my nipples, my soapy stomach and then the round of my cock.

It's a short, one-fingered journey to slip down the crack of my arse – smooth, shaved, my finger slipping up and down.

I don't...

I DO!

I pretend to be fucked with my arse in the air and my cheek against the cold of the tiles, water running over my eyes, impossible to see who it is, who could be ramming it in so hard?

SO!

HARD!

Out. Towelled. New. Clean.

Moisturise.

Moisturise again.

Look at myself. Naked. Lovely. That's lovely there. That bit's lovely. Pose. Look at myself.

Shit.

Shit *me*!

It's one of those nights. One of those. Oh Jesus!

I look like I've caught a star between my teeth and I'm just blazing with it.

Good night for a fuck. Feel like a fuck.

First things first. Harness it. Be simple. Just underwear. Easy. I slip on a pair of Calvins and I feel this sureness inside. Like my planets coming into line.

Trousers on and then tugged down to reveal the waistband of my pants, a temptation, even to me.

Consider a wank. Would spoil things somehow. Anticipation better and all that...

Then again...

Before I can make up my mind I hear her.

Radio on.

Mind of its own.

Alarm set wrong.

I don't like Steps, I hate fucking –

Those poofs who put on foundation to hide their fucked up faces and stand on the dance floor like they just sucked a lemon doing the moves to Tragedy, trying to outdo one another as if there were nothing in their heads at all. Nothing at all! I'm not someone you would see and think 'They're gay' but Kylie.

Kylie on my radio.

She makes me dance is all I'll say.

She makes me fucking dance.

Phone a friend, see what time. Where? Who? Could go round for a drink. See you, see you, loving it already.

Dance my steps through the kitchen, kicking up my heels. Through the bedroom and I can see his clothes lying on the floor, strewn around like clues, where he stood, where he took his jacket off. Been home and out already.

Into the living room and see myself in the great big wall of glass that looks out over the city.

It's dark outside and the moon's made it to being very nearly full. Clear skies. The city strung out below. Me up high over it all.

I imagine myself from below, if you were walking and you were just to glance up, just see me in the window. 'Who's that?' you'd think. 'Dancing those steps. Who's that?'

And the telly, where he's left it on, plays silent in the window. Superimposed on the night.

A newsflash they've been playing all day.

The photo of a girl. A school photo.

Bright-eyed.

Blue background.

Smiling out.

It flicks to the dull footage they have.

Her last moves caught on security cameras. Grainy like. Shadowy.

The way she reaches up, takes his hand.

Across the city she's multiplied times a hundred. A thousand.

People getting in from work, opening a bottle of wine, their heads turned towards it. I can see them in the buildings below, families sitting round with their dinner, watching on screen. Every detail.

And I'm stuck, watching her. Imagining that. Imagining what he'll do to her. What it's like. What's that like? ...

I see myself, as if from below, down on the street. Standing in the window. Dead still in my boyfriend's high-rise apartment. A girl's face on the television.

A phone in my hand and I've forgotten why.

I could speak to him.

Give him a ring.

Get him at the top of some mountain somewhere.

That's where he'd be.

Lying with his bike beside him.

Just lying there with his eyes closed.

Waiting for me.

I can imagine that.

The phone being in my hand and all, seems like an opportunity. Not to do anything, not to say anything special. Just to see him. Maybe. Tell him I want him. Tell him I'm home.

On screen she opens the door. Gets in the passenger seat. The car drives off.

I turn off the lights. Slip out unseen.

6.

The CCTV control room. **PAULA** *is watching a monitor, over her shoulder a* **POLICEMAN** *is watching as well. They watch until the footage ends.*

POLICEMAN That's it?

PAULA Yes.

POLICEMAN Not much is it?

PAULA No.

POLICEMAN There's nothing more?

PAULA No.

POLICEMAN And that's normal, is it?

PAULA What?

POLICEMAN Just to disappear like that?

PAULA ...

POLICEMAN I mean no sightings. Nothing on tape.

PAULA No.

No, it's not normal. I don't know what it is. There's a camera at the end of this street. He should come up on that, but I've checked. I've checked it for the whole day. This is all there is.

They both look at the monitor.

POLICEMAN It's funny isn't it. I mean it looks so...

PAULA What?

POLICEMAN Well...normal.

I mean if you saw that you wouldn't bat an eye. You'd probably smile. We're trained to smile, puts people at their ease. But if I saw that I might actually smile. Man with his daughter. Nothing suspicious there.

PAULA Is that all you came for?

POLICEMAN What?

PAULA Did you want anything?

POLICEMAN Yeah. I've been sent up – Well, my partner's been sent up, but he had to go to the chemist, so I said I'd come and pick up the tapes.

PAULA I've sent it. They've got a copy.

POLICEMAN No, they want all the tapes. From all the cameras.

PAULA Why?

POLICEMAN Evidence. We'll need to look thought them ourselves. Poor bastard, looking through all them. Me probably. Poor bastard.

PAULA But I've told them. Nothing's come up. I've nearly finished checking them all.

POLICEMAN I expect they just want to go through it themselves.

PAULA Why?

POLICEMAN Make sure. Get the experts in.

PAULA There's nothing on them.

POLICEMAN Well, so you say, but / –

PAULA They're wasting their time.

POLICEMAN Well, that's hardly for us / to –

PAULA You're wasting your time. I've been checking everything. Every way out. Every camera. He knew exactly where they were. He's not wasting his time. He's miles away. Look at you. Coming in here. What for? You should be out there. You should be searching for her.

POLICEMAN We are.

PAULA How?

POLICEMAN Dogs. There are dogs out there right now looking for her. And volunteers. Locals, police, the press. They're all out there searching for her.

Especially the press. Love it. The hunt. Divers. They'll be dredging the river tonight.

We've left no stone unturned.

...

...

They asked you to look through the tapes did they?

PAULA What?

POLICEMAN Well, someone's asked you to look through them have they?

PAULA No.

POLICEMAN Oh.

...

...

Knew her did you?

PAULA No. Why do you say that?

POLICEMAN Well, it just sounds like maybe you knew her.

PAULA No.

POLICEMAN Personal.

PAULA I didn't know her.

POLICEMAN It just sounded like it.

PAULA Why?

POLICEMAN It just did.

PAULA I didn't know her.

...

I just wonder if I saw her, you know.

She might've walked past my house on the way to school. They do that. They walk past my garden. Swearing and hitting each other and screaming like...well, you wouldn't believe.

People say they're dangerous.

They say there's gangs you have to watch out for.

But they look just like children to me.

Like they've always looked. Bit raggedy.

Maybe I saw her then.

I do remember a girl. Lovely. Quiet. Maybe that was her.

Do you want my statement?

POLICEMAN No.

PAULA I might know her.

POLICEMAN It wouldn't do any good.

We have to be unemotional.

We can't take statements on that kind of evidence.

"I might've known her."

Then where would we be? Covered in paper. That's where we'd be.

No. We just need the tapes.

PAULA Right.

I'll just...

She goes out. While she is gone the **POLICEMAN** *speaks off to her, doesn't seem to care that she doesn't hear.*

POLICEMAN You like it here do you?

...

It's a bit quiet. I like to have people about. That's why I decided to go into this. I thought, 'Where's a job where you can deal with people, drive about, something different every day?' Well, this is it. Mind you. This'd be all right. I always thought I could do this.

PAULA *re-enters with a large box of tapes.*

The **POLICEMAN** *is looking at the monitor.*

Where's this then?

PAULA It's just up the road. Where the shops start.

POLICEMAN Is it?

...

Oh yeah.

That's just above the snooker hall.

PAULA Yes.

POLICEMAN What about the chemist. Can you see the chemist?

PAULA Yes.

POLICEMAN Go on then.

PAULA Why?

POLICEMAN I just want to see it.

> **PAULA** *begins to move the camera.*

What's that?

PAULA What?

POLICEMAN Go back.

...

That.

PAULA Someone's window.

POLICEMAN Can you point it in?

PAULA Why?

POLICEMAN Just... Go on.

PAULA You can't just do that.

POLICEMAN I know I know. Just point it in.

PAULA It's people's privacy. It's their home.

POLICEMAN It's my partner. It *is*. Zoom in.

PAULA I can't.

POLICEMAN Do it.

PAULA *zooms the camera in.*

He's talking to that woman.

What's he doing?

PAULA Look, I can't...

POLICEMAN He's talking to her. Is he talking to her?

The screen goes blank.

What happened?

PAULA We're not allowed. That's what happens. It just goes blank.

POLICEMAN Can't you get it back?

PAULA Not without permission. Do you want me to get permission? It'd have to go through an inspector.

POLICEMAN No. No, you're all right.

He turns to the tapes.

Is this them?

PAULA Yeah.

POLICEMAN Everything?

PAULA Yeah.

The POLICEMAN exits. PAULA stands motionless. She goes out and brings back two tapes. Puts them in her bag. She gets her mobile phone and dials a number.

Hi. It's Paula.

I know. I know. I'm sorry. I only just got your message. It's been non-stop, I couldn't just leave you know? Yeah. Yeah, of course. I'm sorry. I'll come and get her.

7.

The cottage. STELLA *is in the living room. She goes to the door, calls out.*

STELLA I wanted to tell you. I feel a bit embarrassed. Your television's broken. I tried to turn it on when you were out. Nothing.

DAVID *has come in through a different door.*

DAVID I don't watch it much.

STELLA I hope it wasn't me. Only it might've been me.

DAVID *hands her a worn towel.*

DAVID Do you want some clothes? I've got –

STELLA Do you have another telly?

DAVID No.

STELLA Most people would.

DAVID I listen to the radio.

STELLA You don't like the telly?

DAVID Don't mind.

STELLA You've never tried it much?

DAVID A bit.
  Listen –

STELLA I don't suppose you'd recognise me then.

DAVID How?

STELLA Not that you would anyway, but do you think I'm the kind of person who'd be on television?

DAVID I don't know.

STELLA Well, obviously not tonight. I look awful, but if I were dry. Imagine me dry if you can.

DAVID It's not something –

STELLA Of course. You don't watch much telly I expect.

DAVID No.

STELLA No, it's totally unfair of me to ask.

Beat.

But can you imagine me on screen? Do you think I could do that? Go on, look at me.

Do I look like that sort of person?

DAVID I don't know.

STELLA Try. Please.

DAVID You look... I don't know what you mean.

STELLA Of course not, I said that didn't I, more cultured I expect, the radio. What is it? Radio Four? The World Service? Do they still do that?

DAVID Look, I think –

STELLA I'm on it.

DAVID Are you?

STELLA The TV.

DAVID Right.

STELLA Shopping.

DAVID *doesn't understand.*

I do the shopping channel. Present things.

She watches his reaction.

I know it's not much. Probably you'd laugh, but it's good. I'm enjoying it. It's a foot on the ladder. Loads of people start like that. It's just a foot in the door.

DAVID People do that do they? Shopping.

STELLA It's just like the high street, only from the comfort of your own home. I do jewellery mainly, bracelets and that, limited editions, just trash really, not worth the p and p, but I like it.

It's nice. Hard though. People think it's easy. I would've thought the same, before I was in the business. Do you want to know what the trick is?

DAVID What?

STELLA Smile.

She waits for DAVID's *reaction.*

That's it! That's the trick. They'll do a close-up, you know, of my wrist or my neck, or whatever they're selling and I smile, even when I know it's a close-up, of my neck say, because – and this is the really important bit – you never really know when the camera's going to be on you. That's my secret. That's why I'm good.

Beat.

What do you do?

DAVID Nothing.

STELLA What? No one does nothing.

What about the radio? You fix radios.

DAVID No. Just this one.

STELLA You must do something.

DAVID I don't. Listen, did the police say anything / about –

STELLA I couldn't do that. I'm always up to something. People say that. It's what I'm known for. You're lucky doing nothing. That's lovely.

DAVID It's okay.

STELLA No, I bet it's lovely. Just sit around. Time to think. That's the problem nowadays isn't it. No time, no real thinking going on.

DAVID Did the police say how long they'd be?

STELLA Do you read a lot? I bet you're a real reader?

DAVID Only, I feel like we should maybe try them again.

STELLA I bet you sit in front of the fire and read. All the weather out there. You in here with a novel, or some poetry. Do you read poetry?

DAVID No.

STELLA No. Too much isn't it. Too much to read. I mean sometimes. Maybe sometimes. What about other stuff though. Is it factual things you read? Maps?

DAVID No, look, I'm going to phone again.

STELLA Are you?

DAVID I think so. I think it would be a good idea.

STELLA Right. Yes.

> **DAVID** *picks up the phone. Taps it.*

DAVID It's dead. It's not working.

Was it like this…?

STELLA *(shakes her head)* Must be the storm. It worked for me.

DAVID You definitely got through to them.

STELLA Well, they answered. I dialled 999.

DAVID What did they say?

STELLA They said hello and then I told them I'd crashed and one of them said they would come out.

DAVID Where did you say to go?

STELLA The house.

The bend in the road.

They'll see the lights.

DAVID That was it?

STELLA Then the line went funny. Like he was speaking underwater, you know. Maybe they've been flooded too.

DAVID I doubt it.

STELLA Why?

DAVID They'd have ways to deal with it. They'd have pumps and things. They have to function.

STELLA *has gone over to the dismembered radio.*

STELLA What's this?

DAVID Don't touch it.

STELLA Right.

DAVID It's delicate.

STELLA It's your radio.

DAVID Yes.

STELLA It doesn't look very good.

DAVID It's okay.

STELLA It's all over the place.

DAVID Everything's numbered.

STELLA *(pointing)* What's that?

DAVID It's...it's just one of the parts.

STELLA You can tell me more than that. I'm not stupid.

DAVID It's a diode.

STELLA Right.

What's that?

DAVID It's... It sorts out the radio waves, it's – *(stops himself)* It's not very interesting.

STELLA No go on.

DAVID It's quite boring.

STELLA No it's not.

DAVID Well, when you broadcast something it's sent through the air to your radio and that's the bit that turns the radio waves back into…into whatever, a voice, or a song. Whatever you put in the other end.

STELLA And yours wasn't doing that?

DAVID No. I don't know. Maybe.

STELLA Maybe?

DAVID It wasn't working.

STELLA It's tiny.

DAVID It's delicate.

STELLA To do all that.

DAVID Maybe I should drive you.

STELLA Where?

DAVID To the police station.

STELLA But I thought… I thought I was going to stay here. Do you not want me to?

DAVID I just think –

STELLA What?

DAVID They might be looking for you.

STELLA Then they'll find me. Here.

DAVID But they might not. I just feel like I should do something.

STELLA But we've tried. I mean we've tried the phone haven't we?

DAVID Yes.

STELLA And it didn't work. I think we should stay here.

DAVID You don't want me to take you somewhere?

STELLA No.

DAVID You want to sit.

STELLA Yes.

DAVID Until the rain goes.

STELLA Yes.

DAVID Then I could drive you.

STELLA Okay.

DAVID I'm not used to this.

Maybe it's for the best. It's pretty wet out there. We might float away.

STELLA Do you think I could have a drink?

DAVID What would you like? Tea? Coffee?

STELLA Gin and tonic. I mean, that's what I'd like, but if you've not got it.

DAVID I don't think I do.

STELLA That would have been lovely. Steady the nerves.

DAVID I think there's some beer somewhere.

STELLA Oh, do you think so? A beer, that would be nice. Yes. I'd love a beer.

DAVID goes to exit.

Oh, but do you think I should? I mean with the police and all, they might think it was strange. Woman crashes. Beery breath.

DAVID Well, I could vouch for you. There's no reason they wouldn't believe me. I'll tell them we met and then you had a beer.

STELLA That would be all right.

DAVID exits. We see STELLA look around from the sofa.

That would be lovely.

8.

ALEX 'Would you take my hat' I says as I enter Josie's door.

We call him Josie because he's dosy, it rhymes.

Sitting sprawled on either sofa are the guys.

Tip top every one.

Clean as a whistle.

Sharp cut, every crease been thought about.

Administered.

Wrapped in smells from Envy to Aqua.

Gaultier, CK, Hilfiger, Dune.

Chanel.

The softest sounding most expensive smells.

Sit down, you're making my teeth hurt. Phil grips his glass like it's the last lifeboat on the Titanic and looks at my arse. I can't complain, it's nice.

So, he was kind of okay...

Phil starts off on how he shagged some freaky guy on Tuesday...

Big cock, nice body, would *not* let me fuck him. So I was like okay, whatever, just not very flexible, fine, passed out. *Then*, next morning there's me sitting up at the other end of the bed just talking and he's kind of horny, tuggin' at himself and I'm like fine, not very sociable.

What were you talking about?

I dunno, just crap and then I notice he's edging over and before I know it he's kind of straddling my leg.

Euw!

And then he's starting to press himself against my big toe. And I don't know what to do, so I'm just carrying on talking like it's normal and then he's actually got my toes inside him...

No!

Aye. And he's as slack as an old bag because within a minute, no lube, nothing, he's got my whole foot up inside him.

Fuck off!

I swear! The whole foot, right up to my ankle. And he's moaning and wanking away and I'm just thinking, 'Oh my god, he's sucked my entire foot up his arse,' and that if he didn't cum soon my whole leg could be up him.

So what happened?

Nothing. I just carried on talking and watching him do this... thing. Then it was over and I left. I was totally shell-shocked. Honestly. I got a taxi home, washed my foot and went to bed.

We are splitting, we are waving our hands with glee at the amazing things we do. Every weekend something will happen to someone. Our lives are like glitter just falling.

Then, and I don't know what it is, but something about the way Phil looks at me. And I know they've spent the last hour talking about me.

How's Richard? he asks.

And suddenly they're all straining to listen.

Hushed without meaning to be.

Dying to see if we're falling, crashing, breaking up.

He's fine I say.

Where is he tonight then, couldn't bear to put up with a bunch of poofs?

He's just, you know...

What?

Cycling.

Cycling? Fuck off.

He's cycling.

How?

Who cycles?

Richard does.

But he's gay, I mean he has a car.

He has a beautiful car.

He sold it.

What? NO! not the Audi!

Yep, he's decided never to drive again.

Tell me he's not sold the Audi, oh, it's beautiful.

So where's he cycling to?

Leather interior, air conditioning.

Just out and about.

No back seats.

Just out and about and through the trees and over the hills he said.

No back seats, no fucking kids, that's my kind of car.

How long's this been going on?

He said he was fed up of going out.

How?

I guess he's getting old!

We all get old you know.

Silence.

The rustle of a pair of jeans.

Okay, let's go, says Phil. 'Cos I for one am not ready to start shitting my knickers just yet.

9.

> STELLA *is examining something in her hand. Closely.*
> DAVID *enters with two beers.*

DAVID It's not very cold.

> STELLA *tries to hide the diode. Brings it out again.*

STELLA I was... Looking.

> DAVID *takes the piece from her hand and puts it precisely back on the paper.*

Sorry.

...

I just couldn't resist.

I'm like that.

I fiddle.

DAVID *(puts beer in front of her)* Do you want this?

STELLA You're angry.

DAVID No I'm not.

STELLA You are.

DAVID I'm not.

STELLA Because I looked at it.
I didn't break it.

DAVID I asked you not to touch it.

STELLA I wanted to see. I can't really understand things unless I touch them, you know.

DAVID They're all numbered.

STELLA I didn't take it out of place. I knew exactly where to put it back.

DAVID You know nothing about it.

STELLA So?

DAVID So, it's taken me a week to get it all ready.

STELLA It looks knackered to me.

DAVID Well, it's not. It was ready to go back and now it's probably broken.

STELLA Don't be stupid.

DAVID I'm not being stupid.

STELLA You're exaggerating.

DAVID It's inside you. You're full of electricity. Static. The charge inside a person. You can damage it without you even realising. That's why I asked you not to touch. I didn't say it for a laugh.

STELLA Sorry.

I didn't realise.

Do you really think I've broken it?

DAVID I won't know till I put it back together.

STELLA And then you'll turn it on and nothing will come out and you'll think of me!

DAVID *fiddles with the parts, making sure they're in the right place.*

You're a very practical person aren't you. What's your star sign... No, hang on! Let me guess. You're either Pisces or... Scorpio!

DAVID ...

STELLA No? Cancer then, you're definitely water.

DAVID No.

STELLA No? Amazing. I'm usually bang-on. I would definitely have put you as a water sign.

DAVID Why, what are water signs like?

STELLA Oh, you know, practical...but caring. You're caring aren't you. Not everyone would've let me in like that.

DAVID Yes they would.

STELLA Not some people.

DAVID Why?

STELLA Well, I could be anyone. I could be a weirdo you know. I could have razors in my pockets.

DAVID You don't have any pockets.

STELLA In my shoes.

DAVID Do you have razors in your shoes?

STELLA No.

DAVID I guess I'm safe then.

STELLA Guess so.

So what is it?

DAVID What?

STELLA Your star sign.

DAVID I don't know. I don't believe in all that.

STELLA Ha! You don't even know. When were you born? What month?

DAVID March.

STELLA Pisces! I knew it.

DAVID You said Scorpio.

STELLA I said Pisces or Scorpio.

Give me your hand.

DAVID What?

STELLA Come on, give me your hand.

She takes **DAVID***'s hand. Studies it.*

DAVID What does it say?

STELLA *(frowns)* Oh my god!

...

I don't know. I can't read them.

DAVID *takes his hand away.*

It's all there though, isn't it?

...

Do you like me?

DAVID What?

STELLA Do you like me? I mean, when I turned up at your door. What did you think?

DAVID I...I thought something was wrong. Something had happened.

STELLA What else? What did you think of me? First impressions?

DAVID Nothing.

STELLA Did you think I was pretty?

DAVID ...

STELLA Just first impressions I mean.

DAVID You were wet.

STELLA Not pretty then?

DAVID No. I mean, I didn't notice.

STELLA Really?

DAVID *goes back to the pieces of radio.*

People say first impressions don't count, but they do. They're the only thing that counts.

DAVID I don't think that.

STELLA Yes you do. When I turned up at that door, you thought...

She realises.

STELLA You thought I looked like someone.

DAVID What?

STELLA You thought I reminded you of someone. You said 'You.' Why did you say that?

DAVID Look, I think you should sit down.

STELLA Okay. I'll sit down. But who did you think I was?

DAVID You're shocked still. The shock's making you ask things. It's not a normal conversation.

STELLA 'You.' That's not what you say to someone.

DAVID I was surprised. You surprised me.

STELLA But what were you thinking? When you came to the door.

DAVID You were wet.

STELLA Yes.

DAVID I just thought. I just thought you were strange.

STELLA That's all?

DAVID Yes.

STELLA Not pretty?

DAVID ...

STELLA I like you, you know.

> I'm someone that can tell a person straight away. You know what they call me? Perceptive! They call me perceptive because I'm always right about a person. It's very good in business. The channel say I'm a valuable employee and I know it's because I'm perceptive. When people look at me (and it doesn't matter what I'm showing, you know, it could be a beautiful dress or a necklace or something as insubstantial as a scent) when people look at me they know that it's not going to be crap, and that they might even want it. They might even want it enough to phone up and part with a little money, and it's only ever a little, a very little. I'm good at my job. It's an exciting life.

10.

ALEX Hey! HEY! Screams Phil, flaps his hands.

What the fuck have you got your light on for then you WANKER!

Taxi stops, but not for us. Disbelief on Phil's face.

He stopped for those girls. I can't believe it! He wouldn't stop for us. It's 'cos we're gay isn't it! Do I look gay?

Everyone nods their heads.

Jesus I hate that, it's a total disability, I should get some kind of benefit. 'Camp-allowance.' Not too much, just enough so we can avoid gettin' prejudice thrown at us. Enough so we can shop in Harvey Nicks. We could put it in a special fund and have a bypass built over Lothian Road. A gays-only footbridge.

Josie finds a taxi, flags it.

I'm going to walk, I say.

What?

Phil can't bear it. You must be mad, it's miles!

It's ten minutes.

You might not find it!

We go there every week.

Yeah, but you've never been on foot!

It's hardly a polar expedition.

Well, it might as well be, it's bloody freezing.

Josie understands, knows me better and bundles them in.

But Mark looks at me. You guys go ahead, he says, I'll walk with Alex.

You don't have to.

Please, you don't have to.

Nah, I need some fresh air.

Ooooh, croons Phil from the window, don't do anything I wouldn't do.

Fuck off!

See you, see you, see you.

Takes a minute to recoup and look at who I'm with.

Mark.

The bulk of him grinning down at me from the streetlights, wondering if I'll smile up at him.

Likes me. I can tell.

Let's not stop being brilliant tonight! I hit him on the shoulder, friendly, don't give him any wrong ideas.

Fuck! Let's be all of it tonight Mark.

He smiles like…like that awful smile you can't get away from, thinks friendly is more than friendly. Mental note, don't touch Mark.

Just a moment. That's all I wanted. A moment away from everybody, nobody in front of me.

We're standing by the wall on the bridges.

I hoist myself up and look out, down towards Portabello and the waves there.

My eyes streaming because the wind is coming up from the dark.

Darkness that seeps into the city, washes over Arthur's Seat and laps against the railway station.

A dark that even the lights of a Friday night can't dissipate.

Been there forever.

Mark is still looking at me and I realise I'm probably very romantic right now, looking into the dark like it means something to me, like there are tears in my eyes.

'A boy without a man.'

And he wants to touch me I can tell.

He probably wants to wrap his arms around me from behind, rest his chin on my shoulder and look the way I am looking.

But he can't because for one we'd get our fucking heads kicked in.

Boys in shell suits and trainers itching to slice us.

'Ya fuckin' poofs.'

I like that.

I like it because he can't touch me unless he was mad and most people are not mad.

That takes something special, something Mark hasn't got.

But he wants to. He wants to so much.

Come on you stupid big bastard. Let's go, let's run just down to the end of the bridge and then we can pick on the beggars. Okay?

We can pick on the beggars and push them over and run and hop and skip down to our place, down to our end, where the boys walk hand in hand and everyone looks at you.

Measures you up.

Wonders if they'll fall in love tonight.

11.

Nighttime. Paula's living room. **PAULA** *enters from the bedroom in her nightie and dressing gown. On top of the TV are two videos. She puts one in the machine, then turns out the lights and watches it.* It is footage of an empty street at night. She fast forwards through it and stops it. She remembers something and goes and plugs in the baby monitor. She listens. She turns it right up. It is the sound of a baby breathing. She listens. She puts in the final video and starts to fast forward though it. The baby starts to cry.* **PAULA** *ignores it at first, then goes to the baby monitor, picks it up. The video comes to an end and goes blank.* **PAULA** *is still. She turns the baby monitor right down.*

---

*A licence to produce A Girl In A Car With A Man does not include a performance license for any third-party or copyrighted recordings. Licensees should create their own.

12.

DAVID *and* **STELLA**. *The living room.* **STELLA**'s *beer is empty, she has another one.* **DAVID** *is at his radio.*

STELLA *(looking at photos on the wall)* Who did these?

DAVID ...
Me.

STELLA They're good. They're good aren't they.

DAVID A bit immature.

STELLA Really?
No. I think they're good.
Is that...? That's you. My God.

DAVID I know.

STELLA You look so different. Look at your hair.

DAVID I was a punk.

STELLA Really?

DAVID It was art college. We were all punks.

STELLA You were at art college?

DAVID Yes.

STELLA You're a painter.

DAVID Photographer. I did photography.

STELLA And you let me sit and waffle on about what I do. You must've been laughing.

DAVID No.

STELLA Where's your stuff? Where's your studio?

DAVID I don't have one. I'm not... I don't do it anymore.

STELLA Oh.

Were you not very good?

...

It's just that I know a job like that's very competitive. I guess you've got to get the right angles and stuff, to stand out.

DAVID I was okay.

STELLA It's like TV. So many people want it, but if you've not got it then...

DAVID I was good.

STELLA Yeah?

DAVID I was the promising one in college, you know. Destined for things.

STELLA That's it though, isn't it. They're always the ones burn out. Then the real dedicated ones come through.

DAVID I carried on. Won a couple of awards.

STELLA And?

DAVID What?

STELLA Why did you stop?

DAVID Don't know. I just... I didn't want to anymore.

He turns back to his radio.

STELLA *(turning back to the photos)* They're good.

DAVID What about you? Where do you work?

STELLA Why?

DAVID I'm just interested.

STELLA London.

DAVID London?

STELLA Yeah.

DAVID What are you doing up here?

STELLA I felt like a drive.

DAVID You felt like a drive? It's five hundred miles.

STELLA Is it?

DAVID More or less.

STELLA It was a good drive.

DAVID Why did you come up here?

STELLA Don't know.

DAVID Really?

STELLA Yeah.

DAVID There must've been a reason. You don't just drive five hundred miles for no reason.

STELLA I had a hard day.

DAVID You had a hard day?

STELLA *(angry)* Yes. I had a hard day. Okay. Stop asking me things!

DAVID What?

STELLA Well. You. 'Where did I come from?' 'Why am I here?' Why are you asking?

DAVID Well it just seems unusual.

STELLA You don't believe me.

DAVID Yes I do.

STELLA No, you don't. You don't believe anything I say. You think I'm some kind of retard. Look at you.

DAVID Well, what? You think it's normal for someone to drive five hundred miles for no reason.

STELLA Yes.

DAVID Yes?

STELLA No.

But if they did you should have the decency not to ask any questions.

DAVID Fine.

STELLA It's just hard that's all.

It's fucking hard all the time doing that.

All the time being nice and encouraging, encouraging people to buy things.

Encouraging people through the screen.

I can't even see them.

You know I suggested we got an audience. Something we could react to, see how we were doing. But they just laughed at me. Said the whole point was to get costs down. Minimise overheads and an audience is one big fucking overhead. You know?

...

And then there's all the other things we've got to deal with. I've got other things in my life you know. I don't just work.

DAVID I didn't mean –

STELLA I said, I've got my fucking things to do, you know. Things like all the other women do. I've got kids to feed. Well, I would have, and even if I didn't I've got other things, you know? I've got the right to some private life, some time to do what other women do. I've got some right to spend my money, haven't I?

...

I was tired, that's all.

That's all I said.

And then it's all about me looking tired and a bit down in the mouth.

'Down in the mouth.'

Like I was cattle.

Like I had some cattle disease made my feet swell up.

Talking at nothing. I mean there could be nothing in those cameras for all I know.

A Friday afternoon.

Who's watching telly on a Friday afternoon?

And it's a specialist channel.

There could be no one out there. Just me talking to nothing.

The telly's on, but they're in the kitchen, or out in the garden in the sun enjoying things.

A cup of tea in the garden and I'm staring into nothing. Just a big lens on a camera in an empty studio with cardboard walls and a podium made of plaster.

A podium with a pitchfork leaning against it.

And me trying to get something up about it, trying to make something happen for it.

A pitchfork all gleaming under the lights, new and clean, a green handle and a ten-year warranty and they're out the back, probably out the back with a cup of tea in the garden looking at a bee hovering on a flower.

And I'm saying Yes! Yes I love this pitchfork. I love the way it's angled in the soil and I love its coating and its firmness. It'll last you a lifetime.

I'm loving it and sucking it and licking it and really thinking about it, using my mind to think about it, working it up in my own mind, thinking about how *I* would buy it, how it could be pleasurable to *me*...

And then something happened. I saw –

One of the lights or...what was it? Something there...

Brought me right out of it.

And I look around and it's just me and a camera and I'm left wondering where I am. What I'm doing.

I'm left just standing there wondering, this great silence filling the air and the studio manager suddenly fluttering his hands, like he could flutter something out of me, my last breath of air just fluttered out of me for a pitchfork.

I refused to do it.

I refuse to do it!

Pause.

You think I'm strange?

DAVID No.

STELLA You think it's strange to drive so far?

I just... I'd had enough.

Do you know what I mean?

DAVID Yes.

STELLA Really?

She holds DAVID's *eyes. He looks away.*

DAVID How did you end up here?

STELLA I just kept on going. Saw the signs passing and followed one of them; 'North' it said. I didn't know signs just said 'North,' or 'South.' Kind of basic, don't you think? But I forgot where I was and it was good. I thought that when I got somewhere, and it didn't matter where, I would buy some coffee in a polystyrene cup and drink it in the car. In the middle of nowhere. That's just what I thought of. Me, in the middle of nothing.

Pause.

Why do you live out here? On your own?

DAVID I like it.

STELLA Do you?

DAVID Sometimes.

STELLA I couldn't do it. I like company.

DAVID So do I.

...

I moved out here with my girlfriend, originally. She found the house.

Thought it would be good for us. For a family. Better light. She liked the light.

STELLA I like the light in cities.

DAVID The light here just lifts things off the page.

STELLA I like streetlamps. Signs. Bulbs.

...

So, what happened? Where is she?

DAVID She died.

STELLA Oh. Sorry.

DAVID Yeah.

STELLA You miss her.

DAVID I can't really talk about it.

STELLA Right.

Pause.

DAVID It's funny isn't it?

STELLA Yeah.

Pause.

DAVID I wasn't expecting things to turn out like this.

STELLA Me either.

DAVID You know, when I saw you. When I saw you I thought... For a minute I thought she was there. You don't look like her, but...that's just what I thought.

STELLA A ghost.

DAVID Yeah.

Been on my own too long.

STELLA You know, you should take my photo.

DAVID No.

STELLA Go on. I'd love to have my photo done properly. I always thought I could do that.

DAVID No.

STELLA Go on. You could get your camera. Get snapping again. You'd love it.

DAVID I don't want to.

STELLA Look. We could do one here, one over here, one on that sofa. You could –

DAVID No!

STELLA Oh.

  I see.

  Am I not interesting enough?

DAVID It's not that.

STELLA Well what then?

13.

ALEX I stand looking down on the throng and slowly I see where the others are twisted in.

A line running to the bar.

'Hold hands, hold hands, don't get lost!' Phil is screaming. Coyly eyeing up the guys as he pushes his way through.

'Six Breezers please and eh...is that Grolsch on offer?'

Cheers!

Cheers!

Sit down. Check out the boys. Check out the girls.

Tonight I have this star between my teeth.

Makes my words golden and not a bit dangerous.

Selfish like. Grabbing the attention.

I keep hearing what I'm saying and it's funny, really funny.

Totally spot-on.

I keep thinking about me as if I wasn't me.

I think about the way I'm sitting, and I'll change position to look more...

Attractive.

There are one, two, three...five guys around the bar looking at me because I've caught them all one by one on a tiny thin wire that goes out from my underpants to their brains.

I keep them equidistant.

When I speak I'm really sending out tiny messages about how brilliant I am, and the words travel up the wires.

Make their eyes open wide.

The bar is sinking in a great sweeping riptide of sweat and sex and glances.

And it all rubs off.

I'm filling with red and black spots of lust.

But this thinking. I'm doing it now. You have to be careful.

If you think about it then a gap opens up. A space about an inch wide and you see yourself doing it.

All the blinking and the laughter and the looks and you can't enjoy them.

Not unrepentantly.

You end up looking into the gap that's opened up.

Looking down.

Thinking, 'What's down there?'

Fallen off Alex?

Phil slides over, conspiratorial.

Look at them all, eugh, it's disgusting. Like monkeys, sniffing each other's arses, he's cute.

A pause.

So, you and Richard are definitely okay then? He asks.

Fine I say.

Really?

Yeah.

'Cos I mean all this cycling business, it's not right and I thought that if you're finished with him, well, I could be a rock of strength, you know, pick up the pieces of his broken heart. Stick them back together. Maybe hypnotise him.

What makes you think we're finished?

You're here aren't you? That's what you do. You ignore us for months, then you're back. So that's how we know.

Things are getting close now. One guy sits down across from me, keeps glancing at me.

Another one's furiously talking to his friend, pointing at me even.

Pointing.

Fancy doing that.

I feel them, getting closer, thinking, 'This is it. This is my move.'

'Let's go' I say, standing up.

Feel the shiver in the air. The snapping. The loss.

'Let's go! Come on!'

Whinge about finishing their drinks. A great campness to it. Rising camp.

Josie is halfway through chatting up a guy. A boy. All spots and no product.

Leave him, I say.

He, Josie, looks up.

A moment's silence.

Smiles.

You're up for it aren't you? He says.

Aye!

He considers me. Knows me. Jumps up, the boy forgotten.

Look everyone! He's up for it. The whole lot of you creaming in your pants, this man is on fire! He's putting you to shame.

The bar is mainly watching now, some not, some talking, the lesbians playing pool, click of the balls.

'Look at him!'

Josie makes me stand on the table and I strike a pose. The cutest fucking, most gorgeous fucking sexy guy on the planet.

The ones I played with, the ones I didn't, all looking at me. Most electric, all confidence.

I jump down. The guys are up. We grab our coats. We all know.

Without a word between us. Exactly how to move, how to look.

We're being watched. And we love it.

Outside.

It's fucking raining, says Mark, not so pleased with me being so all-round attractive to everyone.

I can't get my shoes wet, says Phil.

Shut up. It's five minutes away, five seconds.

Hello! Gucci! Do you think Gucci cares how long it takes. No, Gucci cares about the pavement turning into a fucking river.

14.

A storm. **PAULA** *is standing on a patch of grass by a road. She is wearing a nightie with a coat over it.*

15.

PAULA *is standing beside the road. A* POLICEMAN *enters.*

POLICEMAN Evening madam.

PAULA Evening.

POLICEMAN Everything all right madam?

PAULA Fine.

POLICEMAN Lovely weather.

PAULA It's pissing down.

POLICEMAN Yes.

PAULA I was just on my way somewhere.

POLICEMAN Are you all right madam?

PAULA I'm standing in the rain in my nightie. I realise you think this is not normal.

POLICEMAN I've seen worse. I've seen better.

PAULA You'll be thinking I'm mad.

POLICEMAN We're trained not to judge like that madam. 'Mad' is a word. Well, it's full of complications. Like poofter, or Paki, nigger, bitch. We don't use those words.

PAULA Don't I know you?

POLICEMAN I don't think so.

PAULA You don't recognise me.

POLICEMAN I see a woman in distress. They all look the same.

PAULA Can they see me on the cameras?

POLICEMAN I beg your pardon.

PAULA On the cameras. Can they see me? Were you called because someone saw me?

POLICEMAN We were passing. I said to my partner. There's a woman there in her nightie.

PAULA You thought I looked suspicious.

POLICEMAN Conspicuous.

That's my partner there. *(waves off)* He's a good man. Pleasant. We spend a lot of time together.

...

I think he's in love with me.

PAULA So no one called you?

POLICEMAN No.

PAULA Why do you think he's in love?

POLICEMAN All the signs are there.

PAULA Like what?

POLICEMAN Heavy breathing. Sideways looks. There's a certain type of smell a man gives off when he's in love. A tone to his voice. It's gentle.

PAULA A certain care.

POLICEMAN Exactly. A certain care. I can't bear it.

PAULA You think it's degrading.

POLICEMAN It's unprofessional. He keeps trying to stop me. In dangerous situations. The other day we got called to a riot. Bunch of football fans smashing up a pub. And I swear, when we got there he locked the car doors so we couldn't get out. Said we should wait a bit. Said he didn't want my pretty face to get spoilt. Said I had a pretty face. Leant over. Looked in my eyes. And locked the door.

PAULA Are you all right?

POLICEMAN Yeah. I'm fine. It just, you know, gets to me.

PAULA See that up there?

POLICEMAN What?

PAULA The camera.

POLICEMAN Yeah.

PAULA There's over four hundred just in this part of town.

POLICEMAN Really?

PAULA You wouldn't think it, would you, but right here, right where I'm standing, it's not covered.

POLICEMAN I did not know that.

PAULA There aren't many places left like this. Blindspots. Most of us can be seen by someone most of the time. If they were looking.

But if you wanted to do something secret.

That didn't take up too much room.

You could come and stand here.

POLICEMAN Only the people on the road to see you then.

PAULA Yeah.

POLICEMAN Where were you going?

You said you were going somewhere.

PAULA The river.

POLICEMAN Really?

PAULA Yeah.

POLICEMAN You could get in the car. We could drive you.

PAULA I was going to walk.

POLICEMAN I could walk you.

PAULA Wouldn't you rather I went home? You see a woman. All alone. Conspicuous. Shouldn't you take her home? Or to the station. Isn't that what you're meant to do?

POLICEMAN I could take you to the station. I could do that. If you wanted.

…

Or we could walk.

To the river.

My partner could crawl along beside us. I don't think he likes the rain.

PAULA No.

POLICEMAN He'll want to be close though.

PAULA Of course.

16.

ALEX The club is massive.

Dancing.

Thousands of people all around us.

Hands punching out. Heads arched back. Epileptic in the light.

This is beautiful! I shout in Josie's ear.

Beside him Mark is looking.

Not above.

At me.

Looking at me that way and before I can turn away he's asked me something.

What? I shout. Too loud. Avoiding his look.

He taps me on the shoulder.

The toilet! He shouts in my ear.

Come with me.

I'm trying to say no. With everything. With my body the way it is and my eyes the way they are.

You'd think he'd realise.

But no, love is blind. I expect everything I've said all night has been a secret whisper in his ears.

Follow him to the toilet.

Inside he puts his back to the door. No one's coming in.

But someone wants to get out and Mark hadn't planned on that.

Moves over. Lets him out.

And one going out is one coming in.

Soon there's a stream of people coming in and out.

He gives up on privacy. Takes me to one side.

You know...I like you. It's a slow start from Mark.

I'm thinking of my watch, wondering what time it says.

How do you mean? I say. All cheery. Refusing to fall into this.

I don't know what it's like between you and Richard.

It's fine. Speed things up. Two-word answers. Three at the most.

It's just...I really like you. I told Josie and he said just to ask you straight out.

Bastard.

Well, I say. Mark, I've got a boyfriend.

I know I know, I know that. But I just thought that blah blah blah and how he's loved me for blah blah blah. His mouth just going up and down, non-stop, slack with emotions.

I can't hear a word and I'm straining to pay attention.

And then I hear him.

Words forming from the general mass.

You don't look happy, he says.

Fuck. Fuck you you fat, stupid shit. Fuck you and your bloody sensitive face, all emotional, tears in your eyes.

I lean in. Kiss him.

He doesn't respond at first. Then it's all over me. Mouth searching. Saying how he knew it. Saying I mustn't worry. Saying he's been waiting.

I pull him to a cubicle. Hands out. Unbutton his fly. Show him what unhappiness is.

But there's resistance.

Stops my hand.

No, he says. Whispers something. Wants it to be special. His hot breath in the cubicle.

Thinks it's special.

Fine, I say.

Just...

Fine.

Out.

Out the toilets and in with the rest.

Find Josie. Gonna sort him out for that. Punch him in the teeth. Draw blood. What did you tell Mark...

Then I see the sparkle of something in his hand. Presses it against mine.

Leaves it there.

Josie, you dancer! How much?

Nothing, he says. Contacts.

My anger evaporates.

Fucking Mark I say. Guess what Mark said? All over me. Tell them all about Mark, how he wouldn't do it.

Special he says.

They laugh. On form again. Back with it.

17.

> STELLA *practices small poses, changing her face a little here and there. She is like a child working out how to present herself.* DAVID *re-enters with his camera.*

STELLA Where do you want me?

DAVID I don't know.

STELLA How about here?

DAVID Yeah.

STELLA Do I look okay?

DAVID Yes.

STELLA This is okay? You should tell me, you know, if it's not. Just tell me.

DAVID It's good.

STELLA You don't want me to put some makeup on? I suppose you don't do that, have it more natural. In the studio they always want you all dolled up, you know? I sometimes put less on though, it's terrible for your skin. They don't like that. They want you to look as much like a prostitute as possible – sells things. They use girls to sell guys things, you know, power tools. And then it's always couples to sell the women things. It's funny that, isn't it? Do you want me to smile?

DAVID It's up to you.

STELLA Right.

DAVID Okay. Now just look at me.

STELLA At you, or at the camera?

DAVID Into the lens.

STELLA Because I never know that.

> *She looks into the camera. There is a long pause.*

Something changes. **STELLA** *waiting.* **STELLA** *waiting.*

STELLA Take the photo. Take the photo!

There is a flash.

Pause.

Do you think it was good? Was it good? I thought it went well.

DAVID *(dazed)* Yeah.

STELLA *is manic now.*

STELLA Don't stop now. Look at you you're getting into it. You're loving it. What about here? We could take one here.

DAVID Okay.

STELLA Or... No no no, that's too boring. What about the carpet? We could use the pattern. You're meant to use levels aren't you?

DAVID Yeah.

STELLA I could lie down, you stand over me. Stand over me.

DAVID *stands over her.*

There, what's that like?

DAVID Good.

STELLA We could get some flowers and I could put them in my hair as if I'd drowned and you'd pulled me out.

She takes off her top. Underneath she has only a bra on.

DAVID What are you doing?

STELLA Do you not want me to?

DAVID I...

STELLA It's because I've drowned. I've taken my clothes off and you've found me and then dragged me out, but it's too late and now all you can do is take a photo of the scene, get it all perfect, all the details.

DAVID I can't do that.

STELLA Why not?

DAVID You'll get cold. You'll –

STELLA I'm fine. I like it. I like modelling. I wanted to do it before the TV stuff.

DAVID ...

STELLA It's just a thing. It's not serious. It's just something I thought of. Because of the carpet. Do you not want to?

DAVID ...

STELLA We don't have to if you don't want to. I just thought it would make a good photo.

DAVID Right.

STELLA You're making me embarrassed now. Don't do that. Don't make me embarrassed.

DAVID You just surprised me.

STELLA Well, that's not my fault.

DAVID I wasn't expecting you to do that.

STELLA God. It was just a photo. Just one photo.

DAVID Well, let's do it then.

STELLA No. No we can't now. You're not right. It's gone now. The mood. It's completely gone. You've killed it.

DAVID It's just... I don't know you. That's all.

STELLA No. I know I know. Look, I know. I do that. It's just I do things, you know, before I think. It was just an idea. It was stupid. We won't do it.

DAVID is looking through the camera.

What are you doing?

DAVID Smile.

STELLA Why?

DAVID You look...

STELLA What?

DAVID Just right.

STELLA Do I?

>**DAVID** *takes the shot.*

DAVID There.

STELLA *(softly)* Was it good? What did I look like?

>...
>
>We could do another one.

DAVID Yeah.

STELLA What do you want me to do?

DAVID Anything.

STELLA We don't need the flowers.

DAVID Okay.

STELLA We'll just say you've found me, in the woods, my hair's wet, see, and I'm lying in a clearing. My skin's white, that's how you first see me. You spot me because you've gone off the normal path, you can't find your way back. The air's still and the water's just hanging off it. You're completely alone and you don't know what to do with this girl you've found, so you look around and do the one thing you can. You take the photo. You get out your camera from its leather case and the click of the film as it winds on... You look at her through the lens and focus on her face turned away from you. It's turned away and you need a better shot. You reach down to pull her head round (**DAVID** *turns* **STELLA***'s head to him.*) and when you do she has her eyes still open. You've heard how dead eyes are empty, but you didn't know till now. They're empty and looking right into the lens, she's staring at your photo before it's even made and then the shutter opens and...

DAVID *takes the photo; there is a flash like lightning. A rumble of thunder. We see water begin to drip down through the ceiling onto* **STELLA** *and* **DAVID**.

DAVID Shit!

18.

The riverside. The river is a torrent. PAULA *stands alone.*
The POLICEMAN *enters.*

POLICEMAN Done.

He said he'd go to the shop. Didn't seem too happy.

PAULA It's quiet.

POLICEMAN It's four thirty in the morning.

PAULA There's no one here.

POLICEMAN Who were you expecting?

PAULA The police. The divers. I thought they'd be dredging it.

POLICEMAN There'd be no point. Current's too strong. Wait till it calms down.

Then maybe.

PAULA I thought there'd be a crowd of people here. Talking softly. A community. I thought they'd be here.

POLICEMAN It's too wet.

PAULA I'd have stood in amongst them and we'd have talked to each other. People don't mind that do they. In these situations. Talking to strangers. A stranger's the best thing. And then someone would have said something and there'd be a silence and they'd have lifted her body out. And we'd have watched. And it would've meant something. Wouldn't it?

POLICEMAN I don't know.

PAULA It would've

...

Where have the boats gone? There used to be boats here.

POLICEMAN They stopped doing that.

...

Kid was drowned. Didn't have a life jacket.

PAULA I read about that. I remember reading about it. I didn't realise it was this river. I thought it was somewhere in Wales. Wasn't it somewhere in Wales?

POLICEMAN Negligence. People were arrested. The man in charge. He was arrested. But they said he'd suffered enough. He'd cried tears of remorse. There were flowers here. Piles and piles of them. Rotting. People felt connected. Like it was *their* kid.

I didn't.

PAULA No?

POLICEMAN I never do. I'm a very unemotional policeman. Got to be. The things I see.

PAULA Did he mind?

Your partner.

POLICEMAN No. No. Well...yes.

I think he's in a mood.

We have been talking a long time. He gets jealous.

PAULA I just didn't want him there, staring at us.

POLICEMAN He does stare, doesn't he.

...

Can I tell you something?

PAULA Go ahead.

POLICEMAN Sometimes, in the middle of the night, we have relations. Of a sexual nature. I don't want to, but...it gets lonely, you know.

PAULA Yeah.

POLICEMAN Then other nights. We can spend the whole time and not say one word to each other. Just sit there. Radio off. Staring out. And we doze. And I'll wake up and I'll have this feeling inside, like stillness, or... I don't even have to look at him. Just sit there. Listening to him breathe. It's...

PAULA You're in love.

POLICEMAN Am I?

PAULA Sounds like it.

POLICEMAN Nah. Nah. I'm not like that.

PAULA You're lucky. It's nice.

POLICEMAN Is it?

PAULA You should tell him.

POLICEMAN ...

Yeah. Yeah, maybe I will.

...

He thinks I'm strange. The things I say.

PAULA You know whoever's watching from that camera. They could focus right in on us now. They could read your lips. Do you think anyone's watching?

POLICEMAN Maybe.

...

I doubt it.

...

Who'd bother?

They'll be asleep somewhere with a doughnut in their hand.

PAULA No. There's always someone watching. They have to. What if someone walked into the river. They'd need to send someone. They'd send a helicopter.

POLICEMAN That's expensive. A helicopter. I'm not sure they'd send that. More likely send an ambulance, or a bicycle. Maybe just a bicycle.

PAULA No. No they'd have to get here. They'd get here in time.

The **POLICEMAN** *shrugs.*

You wouldn't just disappear.

Pause.

I'm going in.

POLICEMAN Do you think that's wise?

PAULA They'll come.

POLICEMAN You don't want me to save you? I'd be quicker than a bicycle.

PAULA No.

The POLICEMAN *looks at her.*

POLICEMAN Right.

PAULA *walks off into the river.*

Right.

He exits.

19.

ALEX Alex.

Alex dancing.

Alex moving.

Alex the one.

At the bar it's all smiles and everyone's tapping Alex and loving him up because we're brothers all.

Even the lesbians are smiling at him and inside I'm loving them. I love lesbians. All of them.

I'm smiling at the barman and they're happy with me, they're so nice getting me the drink, smiling and do I want ice?

Do I want ice?

I would fucking love ice.

They're offering me everything they can.

They're offering me ice, I say to the guy next door – blonde hair, blue eyes, leather boots and a pair of Speedos – he's amazed as well.

I'm talking. Chatting. What we're all on. How high we are. How great it is. I love you. I really do. And you. I really… maybe we should go swimming.

I walk away.

I walk off down the corridor.

At the end there's a turning off, a room.

Must be under the dance floor because the ceiling and the walls are shaking.

It's barely lit, a room of twitching limbs. Body parts all glowing under the lamps.

I'm standing and there's nothing, just dead quiet. Alex and the quiet.

One girl staggers towards me. A girl, vomit, spit stain down her mouth. Out her mouth and down her tongue. Grabs my arm.

Needs me, needs a hold and a steady hand on her back.

Fuck that!

Fuck her hand and her globby sweat-stained face, skin yellow like wax, sick at the side. Imagine licking that off. Her boyfriend or her girlfriend fucked out their faces, licking each other like that.

I can't take my eyes off her.

She's a treat to watch.

Something powerful in her hold.

Her gob opens, her filthy gob and she's trying to say something. What? What?

'Help me!'

This 'Help me,' this little 'Help me.' Like a girl.

I sit her down. Sit beside her.

But she's a bag of bones. Won't rest where you put them. She's flopping around.

Knees and arms everywhere. I'm trying to get her together, like a game for me, buckaroo.

Her leg slides out. Fuck.

I'm bending over to pull her leg in when she stops.

Still.

From where I'm leaning I can see up her skirt. Knickers and a tuft of hair crawling round the edge.

I want to turn round. Look her in the eye.

But I pause.

Her knee is all I can see – pink, dirty, just a girl really. Fourteen, fifteen.

Feel up her skirt, the inside.

Draw my hand round to the inside and touch with the tips of my fingers where her knickers are.

Between her knickers and the skin.

There.

Touch.

What's it like?

What's that like?

Running now. Not running. Just walking pretty fast. Back down the hall. Back to the guys.

I'm smiling.

Alex! Alex! I hear Mark calling me, but he wants special. Fuck that.

I want dancing. I want to dance.

I want to begin again. And so we do. We begin over and over and each climax seems like it will be our last, my body will disappear and finally…finally I might fly.

God, I say, I'd like to fly.

And I think he hears you know. After all the shit I think that's what happened next because I wasn't on the floor with the mass still grouping and ungrouping.

I was away.

And the clarity, the silence.

My lips parting, forgive me father. Forgive me everything! I say in the silence. And do you know? I feel the grace of God.

And it is…

…

…

And then I see her, on screen, on the big screen above the silhouetted heads of hundreds of dancers, breaking up, a film.

They're playing a film.

The girl.

Crossing towards the car, her hand in his hand.

Giant.

Looming above the outstretched arms of the crowd.

Everyone dancing, over and over, roaring with the kill. Desperate for the end. The finale. Her mangled body. Her burnt clothes.

What are we doing?

I look for the others. Josie. Phil. John. Even Mark. Especially Mark. But they're gone. All dancing somewhere. All alone I feel. Terribly alone.

20.

The loft of David's cottage. The place is pitch-black, the sound of dripping water. A trapdoor opens and light from the rest of the cottage streams up. The loft is filled with camera equipment. Tripods, stools, flash umbrellas.

STELLA What's all this?

DAVID The stuff I used. For my photos.

STELLA Why's it up here?

DAVID Can you give us a hand.

> STELLA *ignores him. Picks up a photo album. Opens it.*
> DAVID *tries frantically to stop the leaking.*

STELLA Who's this?

DAVID *(knocking over a tin collecting water)* Shit!

STELLA It's her isn't it?

> DAVID *realises what she is looking at. Stops.*

DAVID You're looking at my personal things.

STELLA Yes.

DAVID That's her.

STELLA She's...beautiful.

DAVID She liked having her photo taken.

STELLA They're good aren't they?

DAVID They're the best I've taken. Before I knew she was ill.

STELLA I shouldn't've looked.

DAVID No. It's okay. Look at them.

STELLA I'll put them back.

DAVID No. Go on. Have a look.

You're the first person that's seen them.

He comes over to her. Looks at the photos.

Yeah, that's –

…

No.

No, turn over.

STELLA *turns the page.*

Yeah, this is where we –

…

That's not really –

…

Turn over.

STELLA *turns the page.*

Keep going.

STELLA I want to see them.

DAVID No. Turn over.

STELLA *turns the page.*

And again.

STELLA Let me see her.

DAVID *takes the album back off her.*

DAVID Look at them.

She wasn't like this.

He turns the pages as he speaks.

She was –

We used to walk up here.

You can't really see it, but from the top it was just… This view.

That's not it.

That's not what it was like. She was –

You can't see it, but she was always doing something. She was always on the move. She wasn't still, like this. She was –

He turns the pages.

That's not it.

She wasn't like that.

...

Look at her.

There's me trying to get her. Pointing this camera. Trying to catch her.

And all the time she's gone.

I missed her. She slipped away round the side.

Somewhere else.

...

I wish I'd looked at her more, you know. Just seen her.

I wish I'd seen her properly. What she was.

She was beautiful.

STELLA Shhhh.

DAVID I'm sorry. I'm being stupid.

STELLA Yes.

DAVID Only sometimes…I don't remember everything about her.

I remember what she looked like, what she was like, but I don't always remember *her*. And sometimes I don't remember her at all. Do you think that's okay?

STELLA I don't know.

DAVID She used to do this thing. This thing that was *so* her. What was it? What was it? Something with her, with her voice and her…she used to do this…it was just a tone of voice or a…what was it? What? …It was so her it was so…

STELLA Tell me what she was like?

DAVID What?

STELLA Tell me what she looked like.

DAVID She was...well, it's hard isn't it. I mean as soon as you say something it doesn't sound right. She had brown hair, but that sounds so...it's not right...it wasn't like that. It was all different colours. I expect each strand was a slightly different colour.

STELLA What about her clothes? What did she wear?

DAVID I can't...

STELLA Close your eyes.

> DAVID *closes his eyes.*

What did she wear?

DAVID Red, she liked red. Wrapped herself in it.

STELLA And her hair?

DAVID Her hair was...it was brown, every strand a different brown.

STELLA And its smell?

DAVID Her shampoo.

STELLA And her hands?

DAVID They were warm. Mine were cold and hers were always warm.

STELLA You remember her?

DAVID Yeah.

STELLA What was she like to touch? You touched her?

DAVID Yes.

STELLA What was that like?

DAVID It was good.

STELLA And to kiss. What did that feel like?

DAVID We kissed.

STELLA How? Go on.

DAVID I don't...

    STELLA *puts his arm round her waist.*

STELLA Was she like this?

    DAVID *opens his eyes. They look at each other.*

DAVID Yes.

STELLA Close your eyes.

    She moves against him.

    And this? How's this?

DAVID Yes.

STELLA What was she like to touch?

DAVID She was...

STELLA Touch her.

    DAVID *puts his hand to her face. Touches her softly. After a moment,* STELLA *slowly takes his hand and puts it to her breast. Then her crotch on the outside of her skirt.* DAVID *moves his hand inside her skirt, then pulls away, opening his eyes.*

DAVID What are you doing?

STELLA What?

DAVID What was that?

STELLA What?

DAVID That. What did you do?

STELLA Nothing.

DAVID She wasn't like that.

STELLA Then what was she like? Tell me what she was like.

DAVID She's dead! She's dead now.

STELLA Of course. Look. Sit down.

DAVID You've got no right to do that.

STELLA You're just upset.

DAVID That was my love. She was *my* love.

STELLA I know. I know.

DAVID You don't know anything. You know nothing.

STELLA I do.

DAVID Get out.

STELLA What?

DAVID GET OUT!

STELLA Why?

DAVID I don't want you here. You shouldn't have done that.

STELLA But you wanted me to. You asked me to.

DAVID I didn't. I didn't ask for anything.

STELLA But you wanted it.

DAVID I didn't.

STELLA Yes you did. It's all right. We both did.

DAVID GET OUT!

STELLA ...

Fine. I'll go. Where are my things? Where are my things?

DAVID What?

STELLA My bag, my coat. My stuff.

DAVID You didn't have anything.

STELLA Yes I did. Yes I did. Where've you put them?

DAVID What?

STELLA You think I'd just walk here with nothing on. What do you think I am? Some kind of stupid girl. Some kind of stupid girl who doesn't know better? Just give them to me.

DAVID You didn't have anything. There was nothing.

STELLA Why are you doing this? Why are you being like this? I just wanted to help you.

DAVID You don't know me.

STELLA I do. I know you a bit.

DAVID You know nothing about me.

STELLA Stop it. We do know each other. Look. We're here aren't we. We're here together.

DAVID What's wrong with you?

STELLA Nothing. Nothing's wrong. I just...I don't want to go.

DAVID Why?

STELLA I like it here. I want to stay. Just stay till the police come. Please.

DAVID Why are you here?

STELLA What do you mean?

DAVID Why did you come here?

STELLA I told you. I had a crash. You saw me.

DAVID You told me you'd run someone over.

STELLA It was a mistake. I made a mistake.

DAVID You're a liar.

STELLA I'm not.

DAVID You are.

STELLA Shut up. Shut up. I'm not. I'm not a liar. How could you say that? You don't know me. You don't know what I saw.

DAVID You didn't see anything.

STELLA I did. I did. I fucking saw her. I saw her there. She was there...

DAVID Who?

STELLA The girl.

The one on the news.

They say she's gone missing.

I keep seeing her. I don't want to anymore.

Her photo, that's all you see. Her school photo, looking out, looking ever so pretty.

And we're meant to think ahhh, poor thing. But fuck her. Fuck that. What's so special about her? I fucking hate her. She's everywhere. My flat. The studio. We had to go off air because of her. Because of me seeing her. And now here. Even here in the middle of nowhere. She's standing in the road.

And I went for her. I went right at her. Drove my car into the side of her. Smashed against her hip and watched her flip over the windscreen. Flip into nothing.

Bitch.

I fucking run her over. I fucking kill her. Messing in my head. Messing in my brain.

And now you. Calling me a liar. Saying that. You shouldn't say that about people.

You should believe me. I just want her to go away.

...

And his hands all over her. His hands all over her. I keep seeing that. His hands touching her. Doing that.

...

...

It's not fair. It's not fair.

Why would he do that?

Why would he do that? ...

She stares at **DAVID**. *Long pause.*

STELLA Help me.

DAVID What?

STELLA Help me.

DAVID How?

STELLA Just tell me things. Tell me what it's like to be you.

DAVID I don't...

STELLA Please!

DAVID It's...

It's fine.

I sit here. I fix radios. I don't know what to say.

STELLA You love that don't you? The radio.

DAVID ...

STELLA You love just sitting here. Fixing it.

DAVID No... No, not really.

STELLA What?

DAVID ...It's boring.

STELLA No it's not.

DAVID It is. It's boring.

STELLA It's not. You love it.

DAVID I don't.

STELLA Well... Why are you doing it?

DAVID ...I don't know.

STELLA You shouldn't be here. You should be doing something.

DAVID Like what?

STELLA You should be in Brazil. Or Mexico. Somewhere with a name like that. Somewhere with life.

DAVID What would I do?

STELLA Marry someone. Have an enormous family. Buy a boat. Or have a car that goes super fast. Or a motorbike. A motorbike and the open road. Imagine that.

DAVID Yeah.

STELLA You should.

DAVID Maybe I will.

STELLA You don't want to waste your time here. It's boring. And what about me? What should I do?

DAVID I don't know.

STELLA Go on. There must be something. Go on.

DAVID I don't know.

STELLA Well look at me. Look at me.

DAVID I don't know.

Pause.

STELLA Yeah.

Long pause. They sit together.

STELLA What am I like? I must look awful.

DAVID You're fine.

STELLA Am I?

DAVID Yeah.

Pause.

STELLA Yeah.

21.

PAULA *enters her living room, soaking wet, breathing hard. She goes straight to the video cassette and pulls the tape out of it, over and over, until there is none left. A moment. She notices the baby monitor. She goes over and turns it up. The sound of a baby breathing.*

22.

DAVID *is in the living room of the cottage. It is dawn. He sits hunched over, fixing his radio.*

ALEX Outside the club the rain has stopped.

The bouncers look at me, see me like a thousand others. Wide-eyed. Staring. I wrap my coat closer as the sweat goes cold. The sheen of it on my skin.

A seagull picks over the remains of someone's chips and up the street a plastic bin bag shakes in the first breeze of the morning. I have to leave. Leave everything behind. Step off into the sunrise.

My back aches.

I walk.

I feel like none of this has happened before. I feel like the only one left alive.

Carlton Hill catches the light, a few columns, golden.

But it's Arthur's Seat I'm heading for.

Great big chunk in the middle of the city.

The grass wet still as I walk towards it.

Great big rock raised to the sky. Like an accident landed in the middle of everything.

It's always closer than you think. Bigger than it should be. All wrong, but funny. In a funny way.

Climb its sides.

Puffed out. Climb some more.

Takes everything I've got. Muscles burning. Heart pounding. Fucked out.

I climb to the top.

And there he is.

Lying with his bike beside him.

Just lying with his eyes closed.

How the fuck he gets his bike up here I've no idea.

I approach, slip on a stone. Fuck! My ankle.

He opens his eyes.

Looks at me, hopping there.

I don't think I've seen him for days.

I don't think I've seen him like this for years.

I'm bloody crying at him. I'm crying and the tears are rolling down my face because I've had a really shit night and I haven't cried for a long time and my ankle hurts.

He takes me like that.

Just wraps me in his arms and I'm out with it all. I'm telling him about the things that have happened to me and the night and the boys and how I never see him anymore.

How I've not seen him because maybe we don't overlap enough.

Maybe we should try harder to overlap. Then there wouldn't be any need to go out.

No need for the parks, bars, saunas, clubs, graveyards.

Graveyards! he says.

Well, yeah, graveyards. Maybe that is disgusting. But I love him.

And I feel a little forgiveness from that. A little respite.

I love you, I say. I love you.

The sun hits his helmet.

The radio comes on. It is the jingle from a morning show.[*]
DAVID *sits. Listens to it. Gets up. Gets his coat. Walks out.*

The End

---

[*] A licence to produce *A Girl In A Car With A Man* does not include a performance license for any third-party or copyrighted music. Licensees should create an original composition or use music in the public domain. For further information, please see Music Use Note on page iii.

**Other plays by ROBERT ALAN EVANS
published and licensed by Concord Theatricals**

Kappa

Kes

Pondlife

Mikey and Addie

The Sleeping Beauties

**FIND PERFECT PLAYS TO PERFORM AT
www.concordtheatricals.co.uk**

Lightning Source UK Ltd.
Milton Keynes UK
UKHW021626160421
382087UK00007BA/534